Whether this was written by your Command, or your Assistance, or only Acted by your Permission, I will not venture to decide. I believe every impartial honest Man will conclude, that either lays me under the same Obligation to you, and justly intitles you to this Dedication. Indeed I am inclin'd to believe the latter; for I fansy you have too strong a Head ever to meddle with Common-Sense, especially since you have found the way so well to succeed without her, and you are too great and good a Manager, to keep a needless Supernumerary in your House.

I suppose you will here expect something in the Dedicatory Style on your Person and your Accomplishments: But why should I entertain the Town with a Recital of your particular Perfections, when they may see your whole Merit all at once, whenever you condescend to perform the Harlequin? However, I shall beg Leave to mention here (I solemnly protest, without the least Design of Flattery) your adequate Behaviour in that great Station to which you was born, your great Judgment in Plays and Players, too well known to be here expatiated on; your Generosity, in diverting the whole Kingdom with your Race-Horses at the Expence, I might almost say, of more than your Purse. To say nothing of your Wit, and other Perfections, I must force myself to add, tho' I know every Man will be pleas'd with it but yourself, That the Person who has the Honour to know your very inmost Thoughts best, is the most sensible of your great Endowments.

But, Sir, while I am pleasing myself, and I believe the World, I am, I fear, offending you; I will therefore desist, tho' I can affirm, what few Dedicators can, that I can, and perhaps may, say much more; and only assure you that I am, with the Sincerity of most of the foregoing Lines,
Your most Obedient,
And most humble Servant,
PASQUIN.

THE ARGUMENT

Phaeton was the Son of Phoebus, and Clymene a Grecian Oyster-Wench. The Parish-Boys would often upbraid him with the Infamy of his Mother Clymene, telling him, she reported him to be Son of Apollo, only to cover her Adultery with a Serjeant of the Foot-Guards. He complains to Clymene of the Affront put upon them both. She advises him to go to the Round-House (the Temple of his Father) and there be resolved from his own Mouth of the Truth of his Sire; bidding him at the same time beg some indubitable Mark, that should convince the World that his Mother was a virtuous Woman, and Whore to Phoebus. He goes to the said Round-House, where Apollo grants his Request, and gives him the Guidance of his Lanthorn for a Day. The Youth falling asleep, was tumbled out of the Wheelbarrow, and what became of him I could never learn.

DRAMATIS PERSONÆ
Machine, the Composer
Fustian, an Author
Sneerwell, a Critick
Prompter
Clymene
Jupiter
Neptune

Phoebus
Old Phaeton
Young Phaeton
Aurora
Aurora's Maid
Terra
Genius of Gin
Harlequin
Justice
Justice's Clerk
1ST Manager
2ND Manager
1ST Star
2ND Star
Columbine
1ST Countryman
2ND Countryman
3RD Countryman
1ST Rake
2ND Rake
3RD Rake
4TH Rake
1ST Chairman
2ND Chairman
Pistol
Tragedy King
School-Mistress
Tragedy Queen
1ST Watchman
2ND Watchman
3RD Watchman
4TH Watchman
Constables, Watch, Fidlers, Lanthorns, Suns, Moons, Whores, &c. &c. &c.

SCENE

PROMPTER, FUSTIAN, SNEERWELL, and MACHINE.

PROMPTER
Mr. Fustian, I hope the Tragedy is over, for Mr. Machine is just come, and we must practise the Entertainment.

FUSTIAN
Sir, my Tragedy is done; but you need not be in such Haste about your Entertainment, for you will not want it this Season.

Tumble-Down Dick by Henry Fielding

Henry Fielding was born at Sharpham Park, near Glastonbury, in Somerset on April 22nd 1707. His early years were spent on his parents' farm in Dorset before being educated at Eton.

An early romance ended disastrously and with it his removal to London and the beginnings of a glittering literary career; he published his first play, at age 21, in 1728.

He was prolific, sometimes writing six plays a year, but he did like to poke fun at the authorities. His plays were thought to be the final straw for the authorities in their attempts to bring in a new law. In 1737 The Theatrical Licensing Act was passed. At a stroke political satire was almost impossible. Fielding was rendered mute. Any playwright who was viewed with suspicion by the Government now found an audience difficult to find and therefore Theatre owners now toed the Government line.

Fielding was practical with the circumstances and ironically stopped writing to once again take up his career in the practice of law and became a barrister after studying at Middle Temple. By this time he had married Charlotte Craddock, his first wife, and they would go on to have five children. Charlotte died in 1744 but was immortalised as the heroine in both Tom Jones and Amelia.

Fielding was put out by the success of Samuel Richardson's Pamela, or Virtue Rewarded. His reaction was to spur him into writing a novel. In 1741 his first novel was published; the successful Shamela, an anonymous parody of Richardson's novel.

Undoubtedly the masterpiece of Fielding's career was the novel Tom Jones, published in 1749. It is a wonderfully and carefully constructed picaresque novel following the convoluted and hilarious tale of how a foundling came into a fortune.

Fielding was a consistent anti-Jacobite and a keen supporter of the Church of England. This led to him now being richly rewarded with the position of London's Chief Magistrate. Fielding continued to write and his career both literary and professional continued to climb.

In 1749 he joined with his younger half-brother John, to help found what was the nascent forerunner to a London police force, the Bow Street Runners. Fielding's ardent commitment to the cause of justice in the 1750s unfortunately coincided with a rapid deterioration in his health. Such was his decline that in the summer of 1754 he travelled, with Mary and his daughter, to Portugal in search of a cure. Gout, asthma, dropsy and other afflictions forced him to use crutches. His health continued to fail alarmingly.

Henry Fielding died in Lisbon two months later on October 8th, 1754.

Index of Contents

TO Mr. JOHN LUN, VULGARLY CALL'D ESQUIRE

SIR,

Tho' Pasquin has put Dedications in so ridiculous a Light, that Patrons may, perhaps, pay some Shame for the future for reading their own Praises; yet, I hope you will not begin to be affected with so troublesome a Passion, when I tell you, I know no Man in England to whom I can so properly dedicate the following Pages as yourself.

It is to You, Sir, we owe (if not the Invention) at least the bringing into a Fashion, that sort of Writing which you have pleased to distinguish by the Name of Entertainment. Your Success herein (whether owing to your Heels or your Head, I will not determine) sufficiently entitles you to all Respect from the inferior Dablers in Things of this Nature.

But, Sir, I have farther Obligations to you than the Success, whatever it be, which this little Farce may meet with, can lay on me. It was to a Play judiciously brought on by you in the May-Month, to which I owe the Original Hint, as I have always own'd, of the contrasted Poets, and two or three other Particulars, which have received great Applause on the Stage. Nor am I less obliged to you for discovering in my imperfect Performance the Strokes of an Author, any of whose Wit, if I have preserved entire, I shall think it my chief Merit to the Town. Tho' I cannot enough cure myself of Selfishness, while I meddle in Dramatick Writings, to profess a Sorrow that One of so superior a Genius is led, by his better Sense and better Fortune, to more profitable Studies than the Stage. How far you have contributed to this, I will not presume to determine. Farther, as Pasquin has proved of greater Advantage to me, than it could have been at any other Play-House, under their present Regulations, I am oblig'd to you for the Indifference you shew'd at my Proposal to you of bringing a Play on your Stage this Winter, which immediately determin'd me against any further pursuing that Project; for as I never yet yielded to any mean or subservient Solicitations of the Great Men in real Life, I could by no means prevail on myself to play an Under-part in that Dramatick Entertainment of Greatness, which you are pleased to divert yourself with in Private, and which, was you to exhibit it in Publick, might prove as profitable to you, and as diverting a Pantomime to the Town, as any you have hitherto favour'd us with.

I am, moreover, much oblig'd to you for that Satire on Pasquin , which you was so kind to bring on your Stage; and here I declare (whatever People may think to the contrary) you did it of your own mere Goodness, without any Reward or Solicitation from me. I own it was a sensible Pleasure to me to observe the Town, which had before been so favourable to Pasquin at his own House, confirming that Applause, by thoroughly condemning the Satire on him at Yours.

PROMPTER

That, Sir, I don't know; but we dare not disoblige Mr. Machine, for fear he shou'd go to the other House.

SNEERWELL

Dr. Fustian, do let us stay and see the Practice.

FUSTIAN

And can you bear, after such a luscious Meal of Tragedy as you have had, to put away the Taste with such an insipid Desert?

SNEERWELL

It will divert me a different way.—I can admire the Sublime which I have seen in the Tragedy, and laugh at the Ridiculous which I expect in the Entertainment.

FUSTIAN

You shall laugh by yourself then.

[Going.

SNEERWELL

Nay, dear Fustian, I beg you wou'd stay for me, for I believe I can serve you; I will carry you to Dinner in a large Company, where you may dispose of some Tickets.

FUSTIAN

Sir, I can deny you nothing.—Ay, I have a few Tickets in my Pockets.

[Pulls out a vast Quantity of Paper.

MACHINE

Gentlemen, I must beg you to clear the Stage intirely; for in things of this serious Nature, if we do not comply with the exactest Decency, the Audience will be very justly offended.

FUSTIAN

Things of a serious Nature! Oh the Devil!

MACHINE

Harkye, Prompter, who is that Figure there?

PROMPTER

That, Sir, is Mr. Fustian, Author of the New Tragedy.

MACHINE

Oh! I smoke him, I smoke him. But, Mr. Prompter, I must insist that you cut out a great deal of Othello, if my Pantomime is perform'd with it, or the Audience will be pall'd before the Entertainment begins.

PROMPTER

We'll cut out the Fifth Act, Sir, if you please.

MACHINE
Sir, that's not enough, I'll have the First cut out too.

FUSTIAN
Death and the Devil! Can I bear this? Shall Shakespear be mangled to introduce this Trumpery?

PROMPTER
Sir, this Gentleman brings more Money to the House, than all the Poets put together.

MACHINE
Pugh, pugh, Shakespear!—Come, let down the Curtain, and play away the Overture.—Prompter, to your Post.

[The Curtain drawn up, discovers **PHAETON** leaning against the Scene.

SCENE. A Cobler's Stall

Enter **CLYMENE**.

SNEERWELL
Pray, Sir, who are these extraordinary Figures?

MACHINE
He, leaning against the Scene, is Phaeton; and the Lady is Clymene; or Clymene, as they call her in Drury-Lane. This Scene, Sir, is in the true Altercative, or Scolding Style of the Ancients. Come, Madam, begin.

CLYMENE
You lazy, lousy Rascal, is't well done,
That you, the Heir apparent of the Sun,
Stand with your Arms before you, like a Lour,
When your great Father has two Hours set out,
And bears his Lanthorn all the World about?

PHAETON
Oh Mother, Mother! think you it sounds well,
That the Sun's Son in Cobler's Stall shou'd dwell?
Think you it does not on my Soul encroach,
To walk on Foot while Father keeps a Coach?
If he shou'd shine into the Stall, d'ye think,
To see me mending Shoes, he wou'd not wink?
Besides, by all the Parish Boys I'm slamm'd,
You the Sun's Son! You Rascal, you be damn'd!

CLYMENE
And dost thou, Blockhead, then make all this Noise,
Because you're sleer'd at by the Parish-Boys?

When, Sirrah, you may know the Mob will dare
Sometimes to scorn, and hiss at my Lord-Mayor.

AIR I
Gilliflower Gentle Rosemary.

PHAETON
O Mother, this Story will never go down,
'Twill ne'er be believ'd by the Boys of the Town;
'Tis true what you swore,
I'm the Son of a Whore,
They all believe That, but believe nothing more.

CLYMENE
You Rascal, who dare your Mama thus to doubt,
Come along to the Justice, and he'll make it out;
He knows very well,
When you first made me swell,
That I swore 'twas the Sun that had shin'd in my Cell.

PHAETON
O Mother, Mother, I must ever grieve;
Can I the Justice, if not you, believe?
If to your Oath no Credit I afford,
Do you believe I'll take his Worship's Word?

CLYMENE
Go to the Watch-house, where your Father bright
That Lanthorn keeps which gives the World its Light;
Whence sallying, he does the Day's Gates unlock,
Walks thro' the World's great Streets, and tells Folks what's o' Clock.

PHAETON
With Joy I go; and ere two Days are run,
I'll know if I am my own Father's Son.

[Exit.

CLYMENE
Go, clear my Fame, for greater 'tis in Life
To be a great Man's Whore, than poor Man's Wife.
If you are rich, your Vices Men adore,
But hate and scorn your Virtues, if you're poor.

AIR. II
Pierrot Tune.

Great Courtiers Palaces contain,

Poor Courtiers fear a Goal;
Great Parsons riot in Champaign,
Poor Parsons sot in Ale;
Great Whores in Coaches gang,
Smaller Misses,
For their Kisses,
Are in Bridewell hang'd;
Whilst in vogue
Lives the great Rogue,
Small Rogues are by Dozens hang'd.

[Exit.

[THE SCENE DRAWS, and discovers the Sun in a great Chair in the Round-house, attended by **WATCHMEN**.

[Enter **PHAETON**.

SNEERWELL
Pray, Sir, what is this Scene to represent?

MACHINE
Sir, this is the Palace of the Sun.

FUSTIAN
It looks as like the Round-house as ever I saw anything.

MACHINE
Yes, Sir, the Sun is introduced in the Character of a Watchman; and that Lanthorn there represents his Chariot.

FUSTIAN
The Devil it does!

MACHINE
Yes Sir, it does, and as like the Chariot of the Sun it is, as ever you saw any thing on any Stage.

FUSTIAN
I can't help thinking this a properer Representation of the Moon, than the Sun.

SNEERWELL
Perhaps the Scene lies in the Antipodes, where the Sun rises at Midnight.

MACHINE
Sir, the Scene lies in Ovid's Metamorphoses; and so, pray Sir, don't ask any more Questions, for things of this Nature are above Criticism.

PHAETON

What do I see? What Beams of Candlelight
Break from that Lanthorn, and put out my Sight?

PHOEBUS

O little Phaey! pr'ythee tell me why
Thou tak'st this Ev'ning's Walk into the Sky? Phæ.
Father, if I may call thee by that Name,
I come to clear my own and Mother's Fame;
To prove myself thy Bastard, her thy Miss.

PHOEBUS

Come hither first, and give me, Boy, a Kiss.

[Kisses him.

Now you shall see a Dance, and that will show,
We lead as merry Lives as Folks below.

[A Dance of **WATCHMEN**.

PHAETON

Father, the Dance has very well been done,
But yet that does not prove I am your Son.

FUSTIAN

Upon my Word, I think Mr. Phaeton is very much in the right on't; and I wou'd be glad to know, Sir, why this Dance was introduc'd.

MACHINE

Why, Sir? why as all Dances are introduc'd, for the sake of the Dance. Besides, Sir, wou'd it not look very unnatural in Phoebus to give his Son no Entertainment after so long an Absence? Go on, go on.

PHOEBUS

Thou art so like me, sure thou must be mine;
I shou'd be glad if you wou'd stay and Dine;
I'll give my Bond, whate'er you ask, to grant;
I will, by Styx! an Oath which break I can't.

PHAETON

Then let me, since that Vow must ne'er be broke,
Carry, one Day, that Lanthorn for a Joke.

PHOEBUS

Rash was my Promise, which I now must keep;
But Oh! take care you do not fall asleep.

PHAETON

If I succeed, I shall no Scandal rue;
If I shou'd sleep, 'tis what most Watchmen do.

[Exit **PHAETON**.

PHOEBUS
No more.—Set out, and walk around the Skies;
My Watch informs me it is Time to rise.

[Exit.

MACHINE
Now for the Comic, Sir.

FUSTIAN
Why, what the Devil has this been?

MACHINE
This has been the Serious, Sir.—the Sublime. The Serious in an Entertainment, answers to the Sublime in Writing. Come, are all the Rakes and Whores ready at King's Coffee-House?

PROMPTER
They are ready, Sir.

MACHINE
Then draw the Scene. Pray, let the Carpenters take care that all the Scenes be drawn in exact Time and Tune, that I may have no Bungling in the Tricks; for a Trick is no Trick, if not perform'd with great Dexterity. Mr. Fustian, in Tragedies and Comedies, and such sort of things, the Audiences will make great Allowances; but they expect more from an Entertainment; here, if the least thing be out of Order, they never pass it by.

FUSTIAN
Very true, Sir, Tragedies do not depend so much upon the Carpenter as you do.

MACHINE
Come, draw the Scene.

[THE SCENE DRAWS, and discovers **SEVERAL MEN** and **WOMEN** drinking in King's Coffee-House.

They rise and dance. The Dance ended, sing the following Song.

AIR III
O London is a Fine Town.

1ST RAKE
O Gin, at length, is putting down,
And 'tis the more the Pity;

Petition for it all the Town,
Petition all the City.

CHORUS
O Gin, &c.

1ST RAKE
'Twas Gin that made Train-Bands so stout,
To whom each Castle yields;
This made them march the Town about,
And take all Tuttle-Fields.

CHORUS
O Gin, &c.

1ST RAKE
'Tis Gin, as all our Neighbours know,
Has serv'd our Army too;
This makes them make so fine a Show,
At Hide-Park at Review.

CHORUS
O Gin, &c.

1ST RAKE
But what I hope will change your Notes,
And make your Anger sleep;
Consider, none can bribe his Votes
With Liquor half so cheap.

CHORUS
O Gin, &c.

FUSTIAN
I suppose, Sir, you took a Cup of Gin to inspire you to write this fine Song.

[During the Song, **HARLEQUIN**, and picks Pockets. A Poet's Pocket is pick'd of his Play, which, as he was going to pawn for the Reckoning, he misses. **HARLEQUIN** is discover'd; **CONSTABLES** and **WATCH** are fetch'd in; the **WATCHMEN** walking in their Sleep; they bind him in Chains, confine him in the Cellar, and leave him alone. The **GENIUS** of Gin rises out of a Tub.

GENIUS
Take, Harlequin, this Magick Wand,
All things shall yield to thy Command:
Whether you wou'd appear Incog,
In Shape of Monkey, Cat, or Dog;
Or else to shew your Wit, transform
Your Mistress to a Butter-Churn;

Or else, what no Magician can,
Into a Wheel-barrow turn a Man;
And please the Gentry above Stairs,
By sweetly crying, Mellow-Pears.
Thou shalt make Jests without a Head,
And judge of Plays thou canst not read.
Whores and Race-Horses shall be thine,
Champaign shall be thy only Wine;
While the best Poet, and best Player,
Shall both be forc'd to feed on air;
Gin's Genius all these things reveals,
Thou shalt perform, by slight of Heels.

[Exit **GENIUS**.

[Enter **CONSTABLE** and **WATCHMEN**. They take **HARLEQUIN** out, and the Scene changes to the Street; a **CROWD** before the Justice's House.

[Enter a **CLERK** in the Character of Pierrot; they all go in. The Scene changes to the Justice's Parlour, and discovers the **JUSTICE** learning to Spell of an old **SCHOOL-MISTRESS**.

FUSTIAN
Pray, Sir, who are those Characters?

MACHINE
Sir, that's a Justice of Peace; and the other is a School-Mistress, teaching the Justice to Spell; for you must know, Sir, the Justice is a very ingenious Man, and a very great Scholar, but happen'd to have the Misfortune in his Youth, never to learn to read.

[Enter **HARLEQUIN** in Custody; **COLUMBINE, POET**, &c. The **POET** makes his Complaint to the **JUSTICE**; the **JUSTICE** orders a Mittimus for **HARLEQUIN**; **COLUMBINE** courts the **JUSTICE** to let **HARLEQUIN** escape; he grows fond of her, but will not comply till she offers him Money; he then acquits **HARLEQUIN**, and commits the **POET**.

FUSTIAN
Pray how is this brought about, Sir?

MACHINE
How, Sir? why by Bribery. You know, Sir, or may know, that Aristotle, in his Book concerning Entertainments, has laid it down as a principal Rule, that Harlequin is always to escape; and I'll be judg'd by the whole World, if ever he escap'd in a more natural Manner.

[The **CONSTABLE** carries off the **POET**; **HARLEQUIN** hits the **JUSTICE** a great Rap upon the Back and runs off; **COLUMBINE** goes to follow; **PIERROT** lays hold on her; the **JUSTICE** being recover'd of his Blow, seizes her, and carries her in. **PIERROT** sits down to learn to Spell, and the Scene shuts.

SCENE, The Street

[**HARLEQUIN** re-enters, considering how to regain **COLUMBINE**, and bite the **JUSTICE**. **TWO CHAIRMEN** cross the Stage with a China-Jar, on a **HORSE**, directed to the Theatre-Royal in Drury-Lane. **HARLEQUIN** gets into it, and is carry'd into the Justice's; the Scene changes to the Justice's House; **HARLEQUIN** is brought in, in the Jar; the Justice, **PIERROT**, and **COLUMBINE** enter; the **JUSTICE** offers it as a Present to **COLUMBINE**.

FUSTIAN
Sir, Sir, here's a small Error, I observe; how comes the Justice to attempt buying this Jar, as I suppose you intend, when it's directed to the Theatre-Royal in Drury-Lane?

MACHINE
Sir, Sir, here's no Error, I observe; for how shou'd the Justice know that, when he can't read?

SNEERWELL
Ay, there I think, Mr. Fustian, you must own yourself in the wrong.

FUSTIAN
People that can't read, ought not to be brought upon the Stage, that's all.

[While the **JUSTICE** and **CHAIRMEN** are talking about the Jar, **HARLEQUIN** tumbles down upon him. The **JUSTICE** and **PIERROT** run off in a Fright. **COLUMBINE** runs to **HARLEQUIN**, who carries her off. The **CHAIRMEN** go out with the Jar.

SNEERWELL
Pray, Mr. Machine, how came that Jar not to be broke?

MACHINE
Because it was no Jar, Sir; I see you know very little of these Affairs.

SCENE, The Street

[**HARLEQUIN** and **COLUMBINE** re-enter, pursu'd by the **JUSTICE** and his **CLERK**.

SCENE CHANGER to a Barber's Shop

He sets **COLUMBINE** down to shave her, blinds the **CLERK** with the Suds, and turns the **JUSTICE** into a Periwig-Block.

MACHINE
There, Sir, there's Wit and Humour, and Transformation for you.

FUSTIAN
The Transformation is odd enough, indeed.

MACHINE

Odd, Sir! What, the Justice into a Block? No, Sir, not odd at all; there never was a more natural and easy Transformation; but don't interrupt us. Go on, go on.

[The **CLERK** takes the Wig off the Block, puts it on, and admires himself; **HARLEQUIN** directs him to Powder it better, which while he is doing, he throws him into the Trough, and shuts him down. **HARLEQUIN** and **COLUMBINE** go off. The **JUSTICE** re-enters without his Wig; his **MAN** calls to him out of the Trough, he takes him out, and they go off together in Pursuit of **HARLEQUIN**.

MACHINE
Thus ends, Sir, my first Comic. Now, Sir, for my Second Serious, or Sublime. Come, draw the Scene, and discover Aurora, or the Morning, just going to break, and her Maid Ironing her Linnen.

AURORA
The Devil take the Wench, is't not a Shame
You shou'd be lazy, and I bear the Blame?
Make haste, you Drone, for if I longer stay,
The Sun will rise before the Break of Day;
Nor can I go till my clean Linnen's done:
How will a dirty Morning look in June? Maid.
Shifts, Madam, can't be dry'd before they're wet;
You must wear fewer, or more Changes get.

FUSTIAN
Pray Sir, in what Book of the Ancients do you find any mention of Aurora's Washer-woman?

MACHINE
Don't trouble me with the Ancients, Sir; if she's not in the Ancients, I have improv'd upon the Ancients, Sir, that's all.

AURORA
Dare you to me in such a Manner speak?
The Morning is scarce fine three times a Week;
But I can't stay, and as I am must break.

[Exit.

MAID
Break, and be hang'd; please Heav'n I'll give you Warning,
Night wants a Maid, and so I'll leave the Morning.

[Exit.

SCENE Changes to an Open Country

Enter **TWO COUNTRYMEN**.

1ST COUNTRYMAN

Is it Day yet, Neighbour?

2ND COUNTRYMAN
Faith, Neighbour, I can't tell whether it is or no. It is a cursed nasty Morning; I wish we have not wet Weather.

1ST COUNTRYMAN
It begins to grow a little lighter tho', now.

[**AURORA** crosses the Stage, with **TWO** or **THREE GIRLS** carrying Farthing Candles.

FUSTIAN
Pray, Sir, what do those Children represent?

MACHINE
Sir, those Children are all Stars; and you shall see presently, as the Sun rises the Candles will go out, which represents the disappearing of the Stars.

FUSTIAN
O the Devil! the Devil!

MACHINE
Dear Sir, don't be angry. Why will you not allow me the same Latitude that is allow'd to all other Composers of Entertainments? Does not a Dragon descend from Hell in Doctor Faustus? And People go up to Hell in Pluto and Proserpine? Does not a Squib represent a Thunderbolt in the Rape of Proserpine? And what are all the Suns, Sir, that have ever shone upon the Stage, but Candles? And if they represent the Sun, I think they may very well represent the Stars.

FUSTIAN
Sir, I ask your Pardon. But, Sir—

MACHINE
Pray Sir, be quiet, or the Candles will be gone out before they shou'd, and burn the Girls Fingers before the Sun can rise.

1ST COUNTRYMAN
I'll e'en go saddle my Horses.

2ND COUNTRYMAN
Odso! methinks 'tis woundy light all of a sudden; the Sun rises devilish fast to-day, methinks.

1ST COUNTRYMAN
Mayhap he's going a Fox-Hunting today, but he takes devilish large Leaps.

2ND COUNTRYMAN
Leaps, quotha! I'cod he'll leap upon us, I believe. Its woundy hot, the Skin is almost burnt off my Face; I warrant I'm as black as a Blackmoor.

[**PHAETON** falls, and the Lanthorn hangs hovering in the air.

[Enter **3RD COUNTRYMAN**.

3RD COUNTRYMAN
Oh Neighbours! the World is at an End; call up the Parson of the Parish; I am but just got up from my Neighbour's Wife, and have not had time to say my Prayers since.

1ST COUNTRYMAN
The World at an End! No, no, if this hot Weather continues we shall have Harvest in May. Odso, tho', 'tis damn'd hot! I'cod, I wish I had left my Cloaths at home.

2ND COUNTRYMAN
S'bud I sweat as if I had been at a hard Day's Work.

1ST COUNTRYMAN
Oh, I'm scorch'd!

2ND COUNTRYMAN
Oh, I'm burnt!

3RD COUNTRYMAN
I'm on Fire!

[Exeunt crying 'Fire!'

[**NEPTUNE** descends.

NEPTUNE
I am the mighty Emperor of the Sea.

FUSTIAN
I am mighty glad you tell us so, else we should have taken you for the Emperor of the air.

MACHINE
Sir, he has been making a Visit to Jupiter. Beside, Sir, it is here introduced with great Beauty; for we may very naturally suppose, that the Sun being drove by Phaeton so near the Earth, had exhal'd all the Sea up into the air.

FUSTIAN
But methinks Neptune is odly dress'd for a God?

MACHINE
Sir, I must dress my Characters somewhat like what People have seen; and as I presume few of my Audience have been nearer the Sea than Gravesend, so I dress'd him e'en like a Waterman.

SNEERWELL
So that he is more properly the God of the Thames, than the God of the Sea.

MACHINE
Pray let Mr. Neptune go on.

NEPTUNE
Was it well done, Oh Jupiter! whilst I
Paid you a civil Visit in the Sky,
To send your Sun my Waters to dry up,
Nor leave my Fish one comfortable Sup?

MACHINE
Come, Enter the **GODDESS** of the Earth, and a **DANCING-MASTER**, and dance the White Joke.

[They Enter, and Dance.

NEPTUNE
What, can the Earth with Frolicks thus inspire
To Dance, when all her Kingdom is on fire? Terra.
Tho' all the Earth was one continual Smoke,
'Twou'd not prevent my Dancing the White Joke.

SNEERWELL
Upon my Word, the Goddess is a great Lover of Dancing.

MACHINE
Come, Enter Jupiter with a pair of Bellows, and blow out the Candle of the Sun.

[**JUPITER** enters, as above.

GODDESS
But hah! great Jupiter has heard our Rout,
And blown the Candle of the Sun quite out.

MACHINE
Come now Neptune and Terra, dance a Minuet, by way of Thanksgiving.

FUSTIAN
But pray how is Phaeton fall'n all this time?

MACHINE
Why you saw him fall, did not you? And there he lies; and I think it's the first time I ever saw him fall upon any Stage. But I fansy he has lain there so long, that he would be glad to get up again by this time; so pray draw the first Flat over him. Come, enter Clymene.

[Enter **CLYMENE**.

CLYMENE
Art thou, my Phaey, dead? O foolish Elf,

To find your Father, and to lose yourself.
What shall I do to get another Son,
For now, alas! my Teeming-time is done?

AIR IV
Thus when the wretched Owl has found
Her young Owls dead as Mice,
O'er the sad Spoil she hovers round,
And views 'em once or twice:
Then to some hollow Tree she flies,
To hollow, hoot, and howl,
Till ev'ry Boy that passes, cries,
The Devil's in the Owl!

MACHINE
Come, Enter Old Phaeton.

FUSTIAN
Pray, Sir, who is Old Phaeton? for neither Ovid, nor Mr. Pritchard make any mention of him.

MACHINE
Sir, he is the Husband of Clymene, and might have been the Father of Phaeton, if his Wife would have let him.

[Enter **OLD PHAETON**.

OLD PHAETON
What is the Reason, Wife, thro' all the Town
You publish me a Cuckold up and down?
Is't not enough, as other Women do,
To Cuckold me, but you must tell it too?

CLYMENE
Good Cobler, do not thus indulge your Rage,
But, like your brighter Brethren of the Age,
Think it enough your Betters do the Deed,
And that by Horning you I mend the Breed.

OLD PHAETON
Madam, if Horns I on my Head must wear,
'Tis equal to me who shall graft them there.

CLYMENE
To London, go, thou out-of-fashion Fool,
And thou wilt learn in that great Cuckolds School,
That every Man who wears the Marriage-Fetters,
Is glad to be the Cuckold of his Betters;
Therefore, no longer at your Fate repine,

For in your Stall the Sun shall ever shine.

OLD PHAETON
I had rather have burnt Candle all my Life,
Than to the Sun have yielded up my Wife.
But since 'tis past, I must my Fortune bear;
'Tis well you did not do it with a Star.

CLYMENE
When Neighbours see the Sunshine in your Stall,
Your Fate will be the Envy of them all;
And each poor clouded Man will wish the Sun
Wou'd do to his Wife, what to your Wife h'as done.

[Exeunt Arm in Arm.

MACHINE
There, Sir, is a Scene in Heroicks, between a Cobler and his Wife; now you shall have a Scene in mere Prose between several Gods.

FUSTIAN
I should have thought it more natural for the Gods to have talk'd in Heroicks, and the Cobler and his Wife in Prose.

MACHINE
You think it would have been more natural, so do I, and for that very Reason have avoided it; for the chief Beauty of an Entertainment, Sir, is to be unnatural. Come, where are the Gods?

[Enter **JUPITER**, **NEPTUNE**, and **PHOEBUS**.

JUPITER
Harkye, you Phoebus, will you take up your Lanthorn, and set out, Sir, or no? For by Styx! I'll put somebody else in your Place, if you do not; I will not have the World left in Darkness, because you are out of Humour.

PHOEBUS
Have I not Reason to be out of Humour, when you have destroy'd my Favourite Child?

JUPITER
'Twas your own Fault; why did you trust him with your Lanthorn?

PHOEBUS
I had promis'd by Styx, an Oath which you know was not in my Power to break.

JUPITER
I shall dispute with you here no longer; so either take up your Lanthorn, and mind your Business, or I'll dispose of it to somebody else. I would not have you think I want Suns, for there were two very fine

ones that shone together at Drury-Lane Play-House; I myself saw 'em, for I was in the same Entertainment.

PHOEBUS
I saw 'em too, but they were more like Moons than Suns; and as like any thing else, as either. You had better send for the Sun from Covent-Garden House, there's a Sun that hatches an Egg there, and produces a Harlequin.

JUPITER
Yes, I remember that; but do you know what Animal laid that Egg?

PHOEBUS
Not I.

JUPITER
Sir, that Egg was laid by an Ass.

NEPTUNE
Faith, that Sun of the Egg of an Ass is a most prodigious Animal; I have often wonder'd how you came to give him so much Power over us, for he makes Gods and Devils dance Jigs together whenever he pleases.

JUPITER
You must know, he is the Grand-child of my Daughter Fortune , by an Ass; and at her Request I settled all that Power upon him; but he plays such damn'd Pranks with it, that I believe I shall shortly revoke my Grant. He has turn'd all Nature topsy-turvy, and not content with that, in one of his Entertainments he was bringing all the Devils in Hell up to Heaven by a Machine, but I happen'd to perceive him, and stopt him by the way.

PHOEBUS
I wonder you did not damn him for it.

JUPITER
Sir, he has been damn'd a thousand times over; but he values it not of a Rush; the Devils themselves are afraid of him; he makes them sing and dance whenever he pleases. But come, 'tis time for you to set out.

PHOEBUS
Well, if I must, I must; and since you have destroy'd my Son, I must find out some handsome Wench, and get another.

[Exit.

JUPITER
Come, Neptune, 'tis too late to Bed to go,
What shall we do to pass an Hour, or so?

NEPTUNE

E'en what you please.—Will you along with me,
And take a little Dip into the Sea?

JUPITER
No, faith, tho' I've a Heat I want to quench,
Dear Neptune, can'st thou find me out a Wench?

NEPTUNE
What say'st thou to Dame Thetis? She's a Prude,
But yet I know, with Jupiter she wou'd.

JUPITER
I ne'er was more transported in my Life,
While the Sun's out at work, I'll have his Wife;
Neptune, this Service merits my Regard,
For all great Men shou'd still their Pimps reward.

[Exeunt.

MACHINE
Thus, Sir, ends my Second and last Serious; and now for my Second Comick. Come, draw the Scene, and discover the two Play-Houses Side by Side.

SNEERWELL
You have brought these two Play-Houses in a very friendly manner together.

MACHINE
Why shou'd they quarrel, Sir? for you observe, both their Doors are shut up. Come, Enter Tragedy King and Queen, to be hired.

[Enter **TRAGEDY-KING** and **QUEEN**, and knock at Covent-Garden Play-House Door; the **MANAGER** comes out; the **TRAGEDY-KING** repeats a Speech out of a Play; the **MANAGER** and he quarrel about an Emphasis. He knocks at Drury-Lane Door; the **MANAGER** enters, with his Man **PISTOL** bearing a Sack-Load of Players Articles.

FUSTIAN
Pray, Sir, what is contain'd in that Sack?

MACHINE
Sir, in that Sack are contain'd Articles for Players, from Ten Shillings a Week, and no Benefit, to Five Hundred a Year, and a Benefit clear.

FUSTIAN
Sir, I suppose you intend this as a Joke; but I can't see why a Player of our own Country, and in our own Language, should not deserve Five Hundred, sooner than a sawcy Italian Singer Twelve.

MACHINE

Five Hundred a Year, Sir! Why, Sir, for a little more Money I'll get you one of the best Harlequins in France; and you'll see the Managers are of my Opinion.

[Enter **HARLEQUIN** and **COLUMBINE**. Both **MANAGERS** run to 'em, and caress 'em; and while they are bidding for 'em, enter a DOG in a Harlequin's Dress; they bid for him. Enter the **JUSTICE** and his **CLERK**; **HARLEQUIN** and **COLUMBINE** run off. Covent-Garden **MANAGER** runs away with the **DOG** in his Arms. The Scene changes to a Cart-load of **PLAYERS**. The **JUSTICE** pulls out the Act of the 12th of the Queen, and threatens to commit them as Vagrants; the **MANAGER** offers the **JUSTICE** Two Hundred a Year, if he will commence a player; the **JUSTICE** accepts it, is turn'd into a Harlequin; he and his **CLERK** mount the Cart, and all sing the following Chorus.

AIR V
Abbot of Canterbury.

You wonder, perhaps, at the Tricks of the Stage,
Or that Pantomime Miracles take with the Age;
But if you examine Court, Country, and Town,
There's nothing but Harlequin-Feats will go down.
Derry down, &c.
From Fleetstreet to Limehouse the City's his Range,
He's a Saint in his Shop, and a Knave on the Change;
At an Oath, or a Jest, like a Censor he'll frown,
But a Lye or a Cheat slip currently down.
Derry down, &c. In the Country he burns with a Politick Zeal,
And boasts, like Knight-Errant, to serve Commonweal;
But once return'd Member, he alters his Tone,
For as long as he rises, no matter who's down.
Derry down, &c. At Court, 'tis as hard to confine him as AIR,
Like a troublesome Spirit, he's here, and he's there;
All Shapes and Disguises at Pleasure puts on,
And defies all the Nation to conjure him down.
Derry down, &c.

Henry Fielding – A Short Biography

Henry Fielding was born at Sharpham Park, near Glastonbury, in Somerset on April 22nd 1707. His early years were spent on his parents' farm in Dorset. His family were well to do. His father was a colonel, later a general in the army, his maternal grandfather was a judge of the Queen's Bench and his second cousin would later become the fourth Earl of Denbigh.

He was educated at Eton where he became lifelong friends with William Pitt the Elder.

An early romance ended disastrously and with it his removal to London and the beginnings of a glittering literary career. Early advice on this came from another cousin, the noted poet, Lady Mary Wortley Montagu. Fielding published his first play, at age 21, in 1728.

Later that same year he journeyed to the University at Leiden, the oldest University in Holland, to study classics and law. However, within months, with funds low, mainly due to his father cutting off his allowance, he was forced to return to London and to write for the theatre.

It was a twist of fate that was to ensure him both notoriety and a reputation that would exceed his wildest expectations.

He was prolific, sometimes writing six plays a year, but he did like to poke fun at the authorities. His plays were thought to be the final straw for the authorities in their attempts to bring some sense of order to an increasingly provocative Theatre. Some of the plays denigrated, insulted, or criticised either the King, or his Government, in ways that caused them to react with their preferred response; a new law. Although the Golden Rump was cited as the play on which the authorities based their need for better regulation it is thought that the constant stepping over the line by Fielding in his own works was the actual trigger for, and target of, the new law. No copy of the play, The Golden Rump, exists today and it seems never, in fact, to have been performed or perhaps even published. Various accounts attribute Fielding as the author and others say it was secretly commissioned by Walpole himself to bring about the conditions necessary to bring the Act before Parliament.

Whatever the validity in 1737 The Theatrical Licensing Act was passed. At a stroke political satire was almost impossible. Fielding much admired – and reviled – for his savaging of Sir Robert Walpole government was rendered mute. Any playwright who was viewed with suspicion by the Government now found an audience difficult to find and therefore Theatre owners now toed the Government line, works only being available for performance after review by the Lord Chamberlain. A process that was to last in England, although greatly amended in 1843, until 1968.

Fielding was practical in the circumstances and ironically stopped writing to once again take up his career in the practice of law. He became a barrister after studying at Middle Temple – he completed the six year course in only three. By this time he had also married Charlotte Craddock, his first wife, and they would go on to have five children, but only a daughter would survive. Charlotte died in 1744 but was immortalised as the heroine in both Tom Jones and Amelia.

As a businessman Fielding lacked any financial education and he and his family often endured bouts of poverty. He did however find a wealthy benefactor in the shape of Ralph Allen, who was to later feature in the novel Tom Jones as the character foundation for Squire Allworthy.

Fielding never stopped writing political satire or satires of current arts and letters. The Tragedy of Tragedies, for which Hogarth designed the frontispiece, had, for example, some success as a printed play. He also contributed a number of works to journals of the day as well as writing for Tory periodicals, usually under the name of "Captain Hercules Vinegar". His choice of name reveals his style. But then again his other later nom de plumes are also revealing; Sir Alexander Drawcansir and Scriblerus Secundus

In 1731 Fielding wrote "The Roast Beef of Old England", which is used by the Royal Navy and the United States Marine Corps. It was later arranged by Richard Leveridge.

During the late 1730s and early 1740s Fielding continued to air his liberal and anti-Jacobite views in satirical articles and newspapers. He was nothing if not passionate and this adherence to principles would eventually have great reward for him.

Fielding was much put out by the success of Samuel Richardson's Pamela, or Virtue Rewarded. His reaction was to spur him into writing a novel. In 1741 this first novel, Shamela, was a success, an anonymous parody of Richardson's melodramatic novel. It is a satire that follows the model of the famous Tory satirists of the previous generation; Swift and Gay.

On the tail of this success came Joseph Andrews in 1742. Begun as a parody on Pamela's brother, Joseph, it swiftly developed and matured into an accomplished novel in its own right and marked the entrance of Fielding as a major English novelist.

In 1743, he published a novel in the Miscellanies volume III (which was, in fact, the first volume of the Miscellanies). This was The History of the Life of the Late Mr Jonathan Wild the Great. Sometimes this is cited as his first novel, as he did indeed begin writing it before Shamela, but it is now placed later. Once again Fielding returns to satire and one of his favourite subjects – Sir Robert Walpole. In it he draws a parallel between Walpole and Jonathan Wild, the infamous gang leader and highwayman. He implicitly compares the Whig party in Parliament to a gang of thieves, whose leader, Walpole, lives only for his desire and ambition to be a "Great Man" (a common epithet for Walpole) and should culminate only in the antithesis of greatness: being hung from a gallows. By now Walpole had resigned as Prime minster after some 20 years. Fielding could now re-affirm political allegiance back to the Whigs and would now denounce both Tories and Jacobites in his writings.

Although Fielding was never afraid to court controversy he published his next work anonymously in 1746, and perhaps with good reason. The Female Husband, a fictionalized account of a sensational case of a female transvestite who was tried for duping another woman into marriage. This was one of a number of small published pamphlets at sixpence a time. Though a minor item in both length and his canon it shows Fielding's consistent interest and examination of fraud, sham, and masks but, of course, his subject matter was rather sensational.

In 1747, three years after Charlotte's death and ignoring public opinion, he married her former maid, Mary Daniel, who was pregnant. Mary bore him five children altogether; three daughters, who died early and sons William and Allen.

Undoubtedly the masterpiece of Fielding's career was the novel Tom Jones, published in 1749. It is a wonderfully and carefully constructed picaresque novel following the convoluted and hilarious tale of how a foundling came into a fortune.

Fielding was a consistent anti-Jacobite and a keen supporter of the Church of England. This led to him now being richly rewarded with the position of London's Chief Magistrate. The position itself had no salary attached but he refused all manner of bribes during his tenure, which was most unusual. Fielding continued to write and his career both literary and professional continued to climb.

In 1749 he joined with his younger half-brother John, to help found what was the nascent forerunner to a London police force, the Bow Street Runners. (He and his siblings were quite some partnership. His younger sister, Sarah, also became a well known novelist)

His influence here was undoubted. He and John did much to help the cause of judicial reform and to help improve prison conditions. His pamphlets and enquiries included a proposal for the abolition of public hangings. This was not, as you would think because he was opposed to capital punishment as such—indeed, for example, in his 1751 presiding over the trial of the notorious criminal James Field, he found him guilty in a robbery and sentenced him to hang.

In January 1752 Fielding started a fortnightly periodical titled The Covent-Garden Journal, which he would publish under the colourful pseudonym of "Sir Alexander Drawcansir, Knt. Censor of Great Britain" until November of the same year. In this periodical, Fielding directly challenged the "armies of Grub Street" and the other periodical writers of the day in a conflict that would eventually become the Paper War of 1752–3.

Fielding then published, in 1753, "Examples of the interposition of Providence in the Detection and Punishment of Murder, a work in which, rejecting the deistic and materialistic visions of the world, he wrote in favour of the belief in God's presence and divine judgement, arguing that the rise of murder rates was due to neglect of the Christian religion. In 1753 he would add to this with Proposals for making an effectual Provision for the Poor.

Fielding's ardent commitment to the cause of justice as a great humanitarian in the 1750s unfortunately coincided with a rapid deterioration in his health. Such was his decline that in the summer of 1754 he travelled, with Mary and his daughter, to Portugal in search of a cure. Gout, asthma, dropsy and other afflictions forced him to use crutches. His health continued to fail alarmingly.

Henry Fielding died in Lisbon two months later on October 8th, 1754.

His tomb is in the city's English Cemetery (Cemitério Inglês), which is now the graveyard of St. George's Church, Lisbon.

Henry Fielding – A Concise Bibliography

The Masquerade, a poem
Love in Several Masques, a play, 1728
Rape Upon Rape, a play, 1730.
The Temple Beau, a play, 1730
The Author's Farce, a play, 1730
The Letter Writers, a play, 1731
The Tragedy of Tragedies; or, The Life and Death of Tom Thumb the Great, a play, 1731
Grub-Street Opera, a play, 1731
The Roast Beef of Old England, 1731
The Modern Husband, a play, 1732
The Mock Doctor, a play, 1732
The Lottery, a play, 1732
The Covent Garden Tragedy, a play, 1732
The Miser, a play, 1732
The Old Debauchees, a play 1732
The Intriguing Chambermaid, a play, 1734
Don Quixote in England, a play, 1734
Pasquin, a play, 1736
Eurydice Hiss'd, a play, 1737

The Historical Register for the Year 1736, a play, 1737

An Apology for the Life of Mrs. Shamela Andrews, a novel, 1741

The History of the Adventures of Joseph Andrews & his Friend, Mr. Abraham Abrams, a novel, 1742

The Life and Death of Jonathan Wild, the Great, a novel, 1743.

Miscellanies – collection of works, 1743, contained the poem Part of Juvenal's Sixth Satire, Modernized in Burlesque Verse

The Female Husband or the Surprising History of Mrs Mary alias Mr George Hamilton, who was convicted of having married a young woman of Wells and lived with her as her husband, taken from her own mouth since her confinement, a pamphlet, fictionalized report, 1746

The History of Tom Jones, a Foundling, a novel, 1749

A Journey from this World to the Next – 1749

Amelia, a novel, 1751

"Examples of the interposition of Providence in the Detection and Punishment of Murder containing above thirty cases in which this dreadful crime has been brought to light in the most extraordinary and miraculous manner; collected from various authors, ancient and modern", 1752

The Covent Garden Journal, a periodical, 1752

Journal of a Voyage to Lisbon, a travel narrative, 1755

The Fathers: Or, the Good-Natur'd Man, a play, published posthumously in 1778

Other Works (Undated)

An Old Man or The Virgin Unmasked

Miss Lucy in Town, a Play, a sequel to The Virgin Unmasked

Plutus with William Young from the Greek play by Aristophanes.

The Temple Beau, a play

The Wedding Beau, a play

The Welsh Opera

Tumble-Down Dick

An Essay on Conversation, an Essay

The True Patriot, a letter

www.ingramcontent.com/pod-product-compliance
Lightning Source LLC
Chambersburg PA
CBHW021950040426
42448CB00008B/1325